A HANDSHAKE
FROM HEAVEN

STORY BY
CAROL S. BANNON

ILLUSTRATIONS BY
MICHAELIN OTIS

BEAVER'S POND
PRESS
Edina, Minneapolis

Illustrations by Michaelin Otis

ISBN-13: 978-1-59298-153-3
ISBN-10: 1-59298-153-4

Library of Congress Catalog Number: 2006928119
Printed in the United States of America
Fourth Printing: February 2011

14 13 12 11   8 7 6 5

Beaver's Pond
PRESS

7104 Ohms Lane, Suite 101
Edina, MN 55439
(952) 829-8818
www.BeaversPondPress.com

To order, visit www.BeaversPondBooks.com
or call 1-800-901-3480.

This Book Belongs to:

_____

Can we touch God?

Can we reach out

and hold Him close?

We can hold those we love,
knowing they are
a gift from God,
a part of God.

We touch His gifts

when we hold a flower,

capture a butterfly,

or hug a puppy.

We can even touch God Himself!

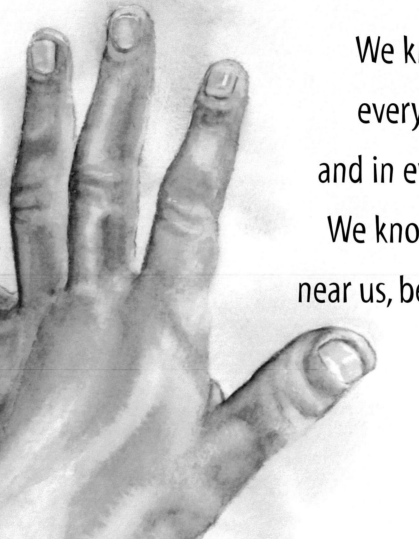

We know God is in
everything we see
and in everyone we love.
We know He is with us,
near us, beside us, and in us.

And we know He is there

in the Eucharist.

For those of us who believe in the Eucharist,

God opens the door to Heaven,

every day if we choose.

And this door leading into Heaven opens each
and every time we receive Him in the Eucharist.

Nowhere else on this Earth
can we touch God.
Nowhere else on this Earth
can we touch a part of Heaven,
for the Eucharist
is His Body.

When we approach the altar to receive the Eucharist,

He reaches out from Heaven's door.

We touch God's Body,

and He touches ours.

We hold hands.

In that instant,

we are one.

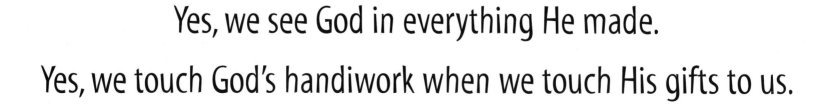

Yes, we see God in everything He made.

Yes, we touch God's handiwork when we touch His gifts to us.

But we truly only touch Him,
touch Heaven, in the Eucharist.

We reach out to receive His Body,

and Jesus reaches out from Heaven's door.

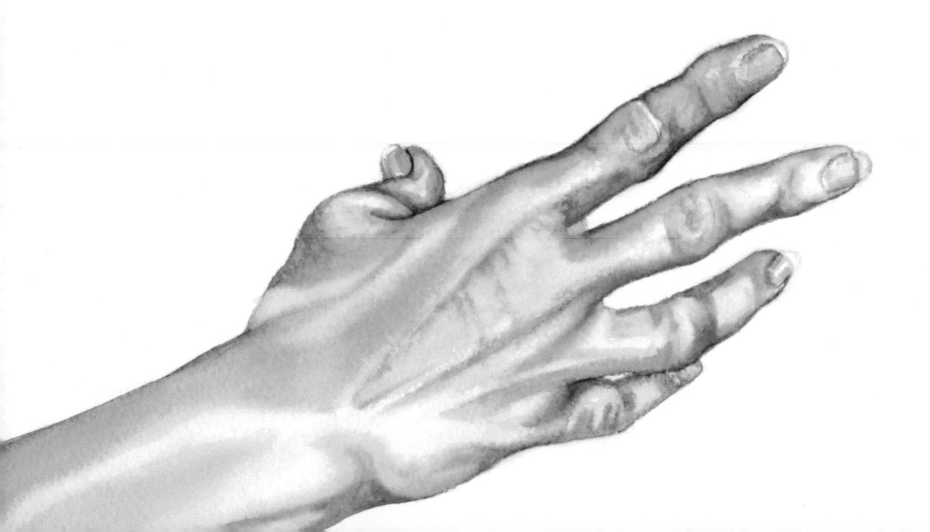

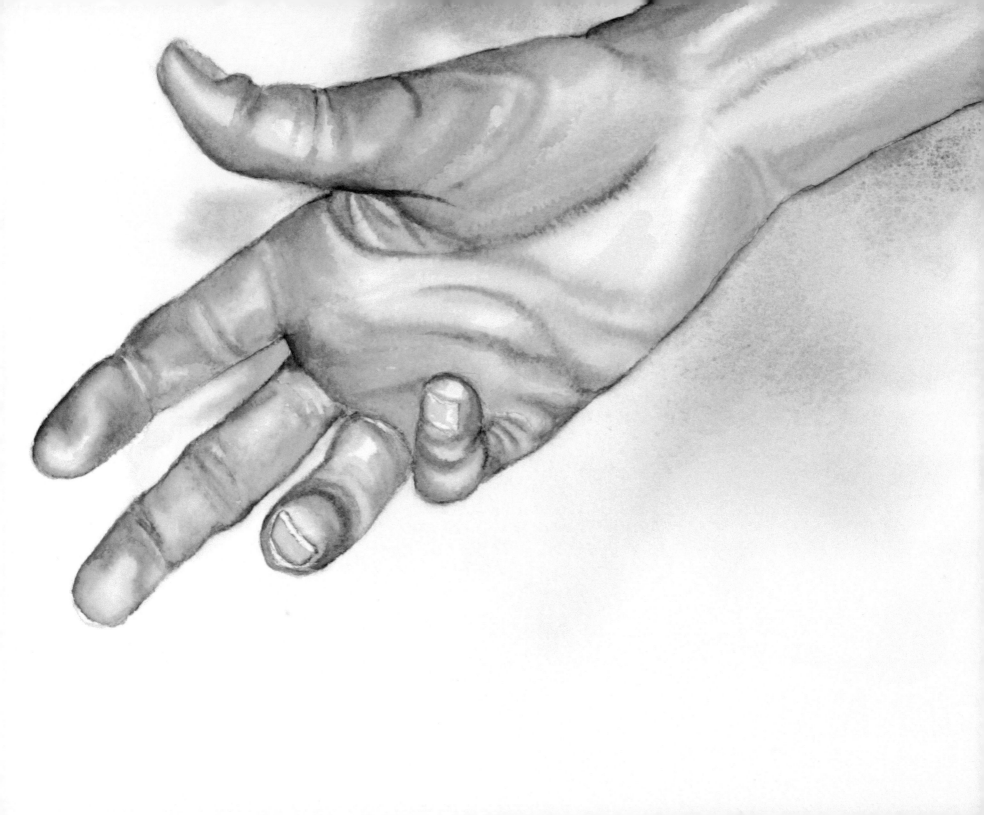

He wants us to reach out for Him.

He allows us to touch Him.

He allows us to touch a piece of Heaven.

This is a gift from Heaven.

Each day we live, we move closer to Heaven's door.
Every day of our lives we can touch Heaven.

The choice is ours to make.

When we choose to hold His hand,

Heaven's door is opened each time.

And on the day He chooses,

we will see the glory of Heaven.

He will reach down for us.

He will touch our hands once more.

Only this time, He will hold on tight.

He will walk us through

Heaven's door.

He will hold our hands forever…

...because we chose

to touch Heaven

while we lived

on His Earth.

About the Author

Carol Sbordon Bannon is a full-time writer with a degree in elementary education from Worcester State University. She is a member of the Catholic Writer's Guild, a substitute teacher, and has been a catechist for over thirty years. In addition to *A Handshake From Heaven*, she is also the coauthor of *Our Family's Christmas Elf,* and a columnist for CatholicMom.com.

She is happily married and currently resides in Concord Township, Ohio.

About the Illustrator

Michaelin Otis is an award-winning artist with a studio and gallery in White Bear Lake, Minnesota. She is the author of *Watercolor for the Fun of It: Painting People* and teaches watercolor workshops around the country and the world. She is the illustrator of *Sara Wants to Know*. She has been featured in many national publications, magazines, and books. Samples of her other work are available at AvalonArtsGallery.com.